To Woo
Staff

BE A BETTER GIFTED AND TALENTED COORDINATOR

It's cool to be clever

Peter Leyland

Best wishes

Peter

22/06/07

Other titles in this series

BE A BETTER GIFTED AND TALENTED COORDINATOR

It's cool to be clever

by Peter Leyland

TEACH
BOOKS

A division of MA Education Ltd

Teach Books Division, MA Education Ltd, St Jude's Church, Dulwich Road, London SE24 0PB

British Library Cataloguing-in-Publication Data
A catalogue record is available for this book

Printed in the UK by Athenaeum Press Ltd, Dukesway, Team Valley, Gateshead, NE11 0PZ

CONTENTS

INTRODUCTION

This is a book about educational change and attempts to show the average teacher how they should act if they were to be given the role of school gifted and talented coordinator. It is not specifically about types of school and subjects, but about able children and how we can improve their ability to learn both the things we want them to learn and the things that they want to learn.

It begins by explaining what an effective gifted and talented coordinator should do and the role they should assume in their school. Drawing on the author's experience, it then goes into how the coordinator should work with different types of pupil, both obviously bright and the underachiever. It continues by explaining the background to gifted and talented education and how the coordinator can find out about and develop the role they have taken on.

An important part of the book is about how coordinators can achieve and maintain the goals they have set themselves. It deals with the importance of making it a whole school issue and the often difficult process of changing attitudes and ideas about ability. It offers ideas about identification, probably the most contentious area for coordinators to deal with, and tries to encourage a broad approach to this. Although we might talk about percentages – 5%, 10% or in some cases 40% of pupils could be considered able in something or other – the book tries to show that every pupil may have a unique gift or talent and that the creative teacher can discover and develop this.

The book goes on to talk about the importance of classrooms, the setting where the teaching drama will be enacted and how we might make them more suitable for the open-ended style of learning that able pupils enjoy. It deals with the importance of bringing colleagues along with the idea, and relating to parents and carers who have concerns about the challenges their children are being presented with.

Finally it talks about how coordinators can keep their heads up in an educational world of constantly shifting priorities and demands. In the words of William Hazlitt, the nineteenth century essayist, the coordinator should 'walk by faith and hope and let the guiding star of their youth still shine from afar'. On that optimistic note I will let you read the book, try out the ideas and see if they work.

CHAPTER 1

SO YOU WANT TO BE A BETTER GIFTED AND TALENTED COORDINATOR?

- First and foremost be enthusiastic. For many colleagues it is just another initiative to be filed away and forgotten about – unless, of course, you keep reminding them about it. Nag them, but don't overdo it – you have to be part of the staffroom too.

- You have to convince colleagues to see beyond the jargon. There never was a more unwieldy title than 'Gifted and talented' and you have to get through the fuzz surrounding this before you can make a serious start. 'More able' for instance might be a better starting point than 'gifted and talented' because it touches a familiar chord.

Between five and ten per cent of our pupils are gifted and talented

This was clearly established by what must still be considered the groundbreaking work on the subject, Deborah Eyre's (1997) *Able Children in Ordinary Schools*. Excellence in Cities says that secondary comprehensives have tended to refer to their top 20 per cent as able pupils and their top five per cent as very able. All its schools were expected to identify five to ten per cent of pupils in each year and this is where we come to a definition of what a gifted and talented pupil is. You may have a clear idea if you've probably been on a state-of-the-art course but if not, here's a list of qualities that fit the gifted and talented criteria:

- physical talent
- artistic talent
- mechanical ingenuity
- leadership qualities
- high intelligence
- creativity
- independent learning ability
- team membership
- social, emotional and spiritual qualities.

It is also worth pointing out that unfortunately, we're stuck with this gifted and talented label and that strictly speaking 'gifted' refers to high ability or potential in academic subjects and that 'talented' means those with high ability or potential in art, music, drama or PE.

YOUR PRIORITIES

Identify the pupils

This is the big issue and one in which you have to take a positive lead. If you're also a subject coordinator in another area, so much the better; your subject can be made a shining example for everybody else to follow.

Investigate the provision

See what already exists in your school – you will often be surprised to find what this turns up. Teachers have a curious habit of keeping things to themselves such as the fact a particular pupil has just won a national chess tournament.

Write a school policy

It's always a good idea to put things in writing. Your work won't be wasted; it gives you a good base to refer to whenever you're challenged, as indeed you will be by one or two less than enthusiastic colleagues. You can always refer them to the policy (have lots of spare copies printed because no-one will ever be able to lay hands on their original!).

Form liaison groups

This can be a difficult one because just like you, every other school's gifted and talented coordinator has at least one or even two other hats to wear. It's best to get someone else to do it if you can, such as your local education authority (LEA).

Involve management

Liaise with senior management, especially the headteacher: If you're lucky the headteacher will already be a convert, or it may be one of his/her targets. If it isn't, then it's back to persuasion again. Don't forget that he/she has even more on their plate than the average classroom teacher. If you're going to succeed in the role the headteacher's support is vital.

The headteacher holds the purse strings. You need money for resources and to buy time to do your job well.

Get the governors on your side

They after all want what's best for the school and it is to them that dissatisfied parents will turn if able offspring are not flourishing.

Involve parents

Show parents that you have a plan for their child – this is the real test of your skills as a coordinator. You have to have answers for them and you have to speak with conviction. This is where the policy is your sword and shield and why you should write your own rather than adapt somebody else's.

Talk to your staff

It's a good idea to ask the headteacher to give you a regular slot in staff meetings, perhaps following on from the report by the coordinator of special educational needs (SENCO), so that you can draw attention to anything you want doing. One advantage of this is that it will be minuted.

Handy Hints

- Investigate current gifted and talented provision.
- Identify the pupils.
- Work with the headteacher.
- Write a school policy.
- Talk to staff.
- Liaise with parents, governors and other schools.

CHAPTER 2

WORKING WITH PUPILS: TALENT SPOTTING

This is the heart of your role and one that you will develop in your own way. For this vital area you will need an up-to-date list of those identified as gifted and talented. It is also best if you know the school and its intake well already. If not there are ways of finding out and exploring methods of developing those pupils who have been identified.

Coordinators can regard themselves as talent spotters, especially if they teach or have taught a large number of pupils at the school. This involves scrutinising the list and seeing where a pupil might be rated highly in nine or ten subject areas. Talent spotting may even mean reading the school newsletter each week and noting sports and other successes. As mentioned before, your colleagues will not always tell you. It is so obvious to them that they think you will automatically know and schools are such busy places the information can often get lost. The staffroom is the place where you must keep both ears to the ground. Although it is more known as a repository of anecdotes about troublemakers, teachers will also talk enthusiastically about successful pupils, especially those in the talent areas of sport, music and drama. If you spot a gifted and talented pupil there are a number of things you can do to develop this:

Mentoring

Mentoring is a method often used to develop the ability of exceptionally bright pupils. Mentors should have some expertise or skill that is not available to the pupil through the school timetable. They can be teachers, older pupils or even members of the local community. Ideally they should have some training for their role and at the very least there should be a method of feeding back to the coordinator what has been achieved in the relationship.

> *Andrew is an example of a year eight pupil that some mentoring was trialled with. Andrew was a very able scientist and mathematician but when it came to subjects such as French he was making such a poor effort that his French teacher referred him to the coordinator. In response, the coordinator set up three half-hour meetings with Andrew and talked the problem through with him. The coordinator already knew a little about Andrew having taught him science when he was in year five. He had always found him thoughtful and able to answer class questions well but reluctant to write anything down. Andrew explained that the problem with French was simply that he didn't have any interest in the subject and didn't know why he had to learn it. The idea of writing out class and homework tasks was completely pointless for him. During the talks with the coordinator Andrew was surprised to find out that he was considered a very able pupil and even more to find that interest was being taken in him from this angle. It would be nice to think that he was also pleased. At any rate his French teacher reported that his interest in French did improve for the remainder of the time he was at the school.*

Group work

Asking the pupils themselves what helps them learn best is a largely unexplored field. Many will cite being able to talk and work with others as their favoured method of learning. Collaborative group work as it is better known has a long history as a means of motivating pupils to tackle ideas that they might find daunting individually. Used as a method with the more able it is like, as Karen Murris puts it in her paper *Can children do philosophy?*, 'thinking with one big head' (Murris, 2000).

Collaborative group work was used with a class of year seven English pupils who were considered to be more able. The teacher researched the group work process with them, bringing in outside observers to record their group discussions. The observer then interviewed members of the group she had observed to discover what they thought about group work.

Responses were generally positive, especially from boys. Adam for example thought that they could find out more about characters in books from getting others' opinions and dramatising the roles of these characters in their groups. Nick thought that the teacher was too controlling of the group work, and this response eventually led the teacher to be less concerned with the product of group work and more with the processes. It wasn't all success, however. Chantelle found the group process a distraction and preferred working on her own. Other girls, however, said that group work made them more relaxed and that the atmosphere in lessons had improved.

Another example was from groups of able pupils in a year eight French lesson. They were asked to choose their own topics. One group chose 'numbers' and asked the class questions in French on things like prices and times, expecting answers in French; another chose to create a drama in which two of them were lost and had to ask another for directions; a third were in a café ordering.

One of the students kept forgetting important words and had to ask the audience to supply it. This created real comedy. Most enjoyed the process, particularly boys like Daniel who thought he was learning more independently of the teacher.

Action research

Often, the best way to get close to how pupils learn is to get involved in action research, which is focused on finding out how changing classroom methods can improve pupils' learning. Although Best Practice Research scholarships have been discontinued by the Department of Further Education and Skills (DfES), there are still a number of ways you can do this. It is a good idea to undertake research with pupils as part of your training for the role of coordinator and courses are likely to provide you with this opportunity.

CASE STUDY

One such course is run by Oxford Brookes University, which I attended in 2000. As part of the action research module, I undertook to see whether by intervening positively, I could raise the achievement of eight pupils identified as more able in a year five, mixed ability science class.

I tried grouping pupils of similar abilities together for the practical tasks that they were undertaking, largely investigative nature in areas such as dissolving and light. I gathered quantitative data consisting of end of topic test scores from three classes. One of these classes was given planned intervention lessons while the others, one of which I also taught, was not.

In the class where the intervention took place there was a significant increase in test scores for the identified pupils from key stage 2 level 4 to level 5. Later I interviewed the eight pupils to obtain qualitative data about the intervention. I found that they enjoyed doing practical rather than written tasks and working with pupils of similar ability but that they were wary about being considered an elite group within the class.

Out-of-hours learning

A school should not be expected to provide everything for the gifted and talented pupil and there is often a need to make use of out-of-hours learning opportunities. Many LEAs now run children's universities or weekend master classes in particular subject areas. There are also evening classes in areas that a pupil might not ordinarily have access to such as fencing or Latin. As the more able pupil is often keen to explore new ideas this is often a good outlet for them.

Helen was the ideal pupil for out-of-hours learning. She was one of a group of girls in a year six Science class who always seemed to have a positive approach to learning. Completing the seasonal diaries, an activity that always lends itself to creativity and artistic endeavour, was always done exceptionally well by these girls.

Helen is outgoing and gregarious but does not have exclusive friendships. It was thought she would benefit from widening her horizons even further and she was offered a children's university place to study drama and puppet making in the summer of 2004.

In September her enthusiasm for what she had achieved was infectious and she was encouraged her to take up a place at an evening venue known as the Frontiers Club. She took up places each term at the Frontiers Club to do an outdoor and adventure sports course and she also encouraged members of the original group to do the same.

Both Katie and Sally, part of the group, took up places on the Junior Masterchef course. This year Helen has been given a further place at the children's university to study food technology.

Pupils with a learning disability

Often pupils with learning disabilities may have particular skills which, because they do not 'fit' into the normal pattern of behaviour, are obscured. Teachers of wheelchair bound, or hearing affected pupils, for example, may find it difficult to allow the pupil to operate independently in the classroom because of the constraints caused by the disability.

David has a form of autism, a condition that made it extremely difficult for him either to relate to other pupils and his teachers or follow the normal classroom conventions. David has a teacher attached to him to give him support in every lesson but was continually breaking the trust with the teacher, causing 2- or 3-day suspensions.

He was, however, exceptionally good at ICT [information and computer technology] in which he developed a skill and confidence that outstripped many of his teachers. Encouraged and guided by an ICT technician, David was able to use his skills in a positive way, assisting teachers in giving PowerPoint presentations by setting up equipment and showing them how to use the technology to advantage in the classroom.

Underachieving pupils

Underachievement is notoriously difficult to spot. Pupils are good at hiding their ability if they don't want you or the school to know about it. There are also those are simply not 'turned on' by school, the most famous example perhaps being John Lennon as noted by Howard Gardner (1983) in *Frames of Mind: the Theory of Multiple Intelligences*. Others just seem to be eccentric regarding their ability and are reluctant to engage in activities that might focus them because of fear of rejection or failure.

Michael is a very able pupil in year six who does not fit in to any recognisable profile. He is untidy in dress and manner, rarely has a pen or a sharp pencil, is ready with answers but mumbles them or goes into so much detail that the sense of what he is trying to say is lost. He is also unpopular with other children to the point that he is often verbally and physically bullied.

The school gave him an opportunity to attend an out-of-hours class on drama through improvisation with the idea that it would improve his self-image. It is too early to tell whether it has worked but he did try it out.

You may have pupils with English as a Second Language who have difficulty expressing themselves both in written and spoken forms. This makes it difficult for them to be identified as 'gifted'.

Born and brought up in Spain, Teresa came to school in England with a good grasp of English from her Spanish school but had great difficulty with reading. Given a National Foundation for Educational Research (NFER) test in her first week of school, she was forced to abandon it unfinished, an unfortunate blow to her self-confidence.

Luckily, Teresa had a natural ability for drama and speaking roles and with the support of classmates and teachers was soon able to establish herself. When shown a CD of herself reading poetry in a group recital, she immediately begged a copy to show to her parents. She repeated the NFER test at the end of the year and her score had risen considerably, putting her firmly into the category of gifted and talented pupils at the school.

Exceptional ability

One or two pupils are exceptionally able, usually one or two per cent. In her excellent book *Supporting the Child of Exceptional Ability*, Susan Leyden (2002) talks about rare cases of unusual ability in children such as the philosopher John Stuart Mill who was studying Greek at the age of 3 years. You may not come across anyone quite so able, but you will meet pupils who stand out above the rest in your school.

John had been nominated as gifted in every academic area of the curriculum and talented in both games and PE. In year six science classes John was challenged, as many pupils are, by the idea of fair testing.

Knowing that the SATs [Standard Attainment Target] tests were now putting greater emphasis on an understanding of the process skills, John's teacher worked on his understanding of the difference between fair testing and checking for accuracy. The teacher also involved John's parents. To everyone's delight he achieved 100 per cent in the 2005 science SATs tests, no mean feat.

There was also something special about Anna in year nine. Anna was a quiet girl who always sat at the back, hair covering her face but whose facility with language enabled her to create astonishingly good short stories about characters like Prunella Wansgate. This story in particular had a mature, controlled style and a chilling denouement. Anna was the kind of writer who you hope would one day rival Jacqueline Wilson on the school library shelves and may even mention you in the TES 'My Best Teacher' series.

Parental involvement

Often the parents of bright children have a skill they are prepared to share with you and the pupils. If this can be arranged, it is a good idea for teacher and parent to meet in advance to discuss and plan the input that the parent can make and decide what the desired outcomes are.

Danielle was one of three pupils in a class whose parents worked in scientific research. Although most were busy people, Danielle's mother, Dr X agreed to come in and teach pupils the use of line graphs, using her current study of fattening pigs.

On the pre-arranged day Dr X came in carrying a life-size model of one of the pigs. This made for a great start. She then gave the class a PowerPoint presentation of how she carried out her work at local research institute. Finally, she presented the pupils with tables of gains in weight made by the pigs using different types of feed. They were then asked to graph these with the teacher, a learning assistant and Dr X assisting pupils.

Afterwards, the teacher reported that the bright half dozen pupils had benefited immensely from the input while the others had been motivated and challenged by the lesson to complete their graphs. When it was reported in the staff room other teachers were keen to try it and Dr X was in great demand.

School trips

Very often a school trip can be the springboard for challenging, able pupils. It might be that a visit to a Wildlife Trust site has sparked an interest in pond dipping or a visit to a local history museum promotes an interest in Victorian dress.

JS Renzulli, in his studies of giftedness (Renzulli and Rees, 1985), talks about the three components of giftedness – intelligence, commitment and creativity. Sometimes a creative spark is needed to start something off.

A class of year four pupils had been visiting Stoke Bruerne Canal Museum in Northamptonshire. One group of five bright pupils, however, were disappointed to find that the coin-operated model of the Anderton boat lift was not working. The teacher had suggested they draw an object from the museum and so Ravi and Sarinder decided to draw the lift.

The teacher observed their total concentration and knowing that she had an advisory teacher coming in to help during the week suggested they might make a working model of it themselves. This idea was received with tremendous enthusiasm by the group and on the following Monday the advisory teacher arrived to help them start.

The advisory teacher set two of the pupils to make the housing for the machinery, one to make the barge itself and the other two to make the frame. The teacher helped them with the construction of the frame and showed how they could use cotton reels as pulleys. He then went off to work with another class, promising to see them again later in the week.

When he returned it was to find that the model barge lift was finished and that it worked. It was Sarinder who had made the leap forward. She had arranged a row of cotton reels, pivoting on dowelling along each side of the top of the frame. She had then assembled a weight system whereby lengths of string were looped over these pulleys and attached to the tank. Aerosol lids had been tied to the free ends of the string and when you wanted to lift the tank with the barge in it from one canal level to the next you simply added marbles to the lids and the strings pulled the tank up. The whole had been set into a model of the surrounding canal system constructed by other members of the group. Even the lift operator's cottage was there.

Pupils and their learning

Alongside the gifted and talented movement there has been renewed interest in learning theories. At the forefront of these is Howard Gardner's idea that there are different forms of intelligence. There are also the theories of brain organisation and thinking espoused by people like Ned Herrmann and Edward De Bono. Although it is not suggested that you base your gifted and talented policy on any of these ideas, it is well worth your being aware of them.

Multiple intelligences

Gardner's (1983) model of multiple intelligences suggests that the concept of ability should not simple be confined to the academic but should include the bodily kinaesthetic, the interpersonal and the intrapersonal. In this way all areas of pupils' learning are involved, such as that of personal, social and health education (PSHE), as well as the more traditional ones. PSHE coordinators might not see themselves as part of the gifted and talented initiative but using Gardner's ideas you can show them that interpersonal skills like leadership, ability to mediate, and building a consensus among pupils, are qualities that have a value that can be quantified in the same way as a facility for languages.

Intrapersonal skills such as the ability to motivate oneself, to pursue individual interests and agendas and to use metacognitive skills, have a strong bearing on how a gifted and talented pupil will develop. Metacognition, or an understanding of how we learn, is a very useful tool for the gifted and talented pupil and can be directly related to learning styles. Although most adults are likely to know their best mode of learning, children and students are still in the process of discovering theirs.

Broadly speaking there are three distinct learning styles, the visual, the auditory and the kinaesthetic. An example of the first might be writing down notes on what the teacher is saying; auditory would be discussing things in order to understand them better and kinaesthetic would having the ability to move around while studying. Not too practical when you have a class of thirty admittedly, but you will get the general idea.

The Myers Briggs Type Indicator (MBTI) is an interesting way of discovering your own learning style. Using this technique (you will probably have to go on one of their courses to do it) you will find out whether you learn best by doing hands on activities, doing hands on activities with others, imagining, writing or creating with others or by categorising, analysing or applying logic. Once you have an appreciation that we all learn in different ways, it is easy to apply this to pupils. When one of them says that the lesson is boring you shouldn't take it personally, it might simply mean that you're using the wrong learning style for them.

Creative brain

Herrmann's idea (1988) about the creative brain is a putting together of two theories – that of the 'triune' brain proposed by Dr Paul McClean, and that of the 'left brain/right brain' of Roger Sperry (Sperry won the Nobel Prize in 1981 for work with 'split-brain' research).

The first of these theories suggests that the human brain is actually three brains – the reptilian, limbic or mammalian (a system of functionally-related neural structures in the brain that are involved in emotional behaviour), and the neocortex (thinking cap).

The second theory says that the neocortex has a left and right half as does the limbic system.

Incorporating the two, Herrmann proposes that the whole brain model shows different modes of thinking. The upper cerebral left area is analytical, mathematical and problem solving while the lower limbic area controls the interpersonal, emotional, musical, spiritual and 'talker' modes.

Respected educational commentators like Professor Guy Claxton in *An Intelligent Look at Emotional Intelligence* (2005) call these theories 'neurobabble'. He says that there is no such thing as the limbic brain and that there is no emotional layer in the brain, which separates thinking from the visceral functions as suggested in McClean's proposition. He also disagrees with the idea that the brain can be separated into two hemispheres, the logical left brain and the emotional right brain, and pours cold water on the ideas of 'braingym', whereby '...touching the ear to the opposite knee for five minutes a day can pupils can improve their thinking...'.

Claxton's book is also a useful corrective to those who would overstate the claims of emotional intelligence in education. At the end of it he counsels that people remember their own lived experience when they step into the world of emotional intelligence so that they do not '...deceive young people or their teachers either about the slipperiness and inscrutability ...of their emotional lives'.

Despite some more research into brain theory, however, I have not yet discovered anything to suggest that it is not useful for children to have a bottle of water with them when they are working in order to refresh their thinking during the lesson. A number of schools in Bedfordshire did some small-scale research into the effect of allowing this and the results were almost always positive. Make sure you tell your pupils, however, that when you are giving a lesson on electrical safety in the lab, then is not the time to take their bottles from their bags for a lusty swig!

Handy Hints

- There are many ways of spotting and developing gifted and talented pupils. These can include mentoring, group work, action research and out-of-hours learning.
- Don't forget to watch out for pupils with a learning disability, underachieving pupils and those with exceptional ability, as they may all have areas of talent which need to be nurtured.
- Parental involvement and school trips can help to stimulate some gifted and talented pupils.
- Theories about pupils' learning include multiple intelligences, the creative brain and emotional intelligence.

CHAPTER 3

KEEPING ON TOP OF YOUR AREA OF RESPONSIBILITY: WHO AND WHAT

WHO'S WHO

There are a number of names associated with gifted and talented education. Although this list is by no means exhaustive it gives a flavour of my own experience of listening and talking to different people in the field.

Deborah Eyre

The first and foremost, I think, in any consideration of the notion of high ability in the English Educational system is Deborah Eyre. Working in Oxfordshire in the 1980s she recognised that the needs of able children in state schools had been generally ignored since the ending of grammar schools. An inspirational speaker and writer, Deborah provided the author's own introduction to gifted and talented education in 2000. At Oxford Brookes University Research Centre for Able Pupils (ReCAP), she directed training courses on Action Research and Able and Gifted Pupils, and Disseminating Provision for Able and Gifted Pupils. These modules could be completed as part of an MA in Education. At the time of writing she is Director of the Academy for Gifted and Talented Youth (NAGTY).

Barry Hymer

Another inspirational speaker, Barry is a senior educational psychologist who has taught in primary and secondary schools. He is an exponent of the thinking skills approach known as P4C (Philosophy for/with Children). A believer in meditative rather than 'fast' thinking, Barry opposes the test and target driven schooling in which most teachers are involved and proposes 'slow schools' in which teachers can let go of prescribing outcomes and concentrate on the processes of learning. His idea of a gifted and talented student is one who has 'reflected on his or her pattern of learning strengths and preference and identified his/her area/s of greatest strength/s within an enriched learning environment'.

Belle Wallace

Belle Wallace, president of National Association for Able Children in Education (NACE), is also a proponent of thinking skills. With an emphasis on problem solving, her books include a series of multiracial learning materials to develop language and thinking.

She has developed thinking skills books for primary and early years pupils, which use what she calls TASC (thinking actively in a social context) to inform lesson ideas. One example of an idea for early years lesson presented at the National Primary Forum in 2005 involved an enquiry into the best place to keep a sandwich fresh for 'our teddy bears' picnic'. Belle is a good speaker and draws attention to the difference between open and closed questions across multiple abilities based on Howard Gardner's model (1983).

Carrie Winstanley

An ex-teacher, Carrie is a lively and exciting speaker who now lectures at Roehampton University. She has written a challenging book, *Too Clever By Half*, about why and how we should provide for the highly able child (Winstanley, 2004). She too has a philosophical perspective and is particularly interested in the able disadvantaged and the able underachiever. Her ideas on definitions are especially good for those of us bedevilled by problems of having to define for colleagues just who we are talking about and, in a section on the meaning of words, she indicates that there is no general agreement on this.

Joseph Renzulli

Teachers being teachers like a comfortable definition to work from. One that I personally have found answers most of my questions is Renzulli's 'Three-Ring Definition of Giftedness' (Renzulli and Rees, 1985), which shows how when above average ability, task commitment and creativity interact, a pupil can be considered gifted. For those teachers who wish to go further with Renzulli's ideas, they might consider his 'revolving door' model by which students can enter or leave a higher level programme as it suits them

Renzulli states, '...If a particular student has a superior potential for performance in a particular area of sincere interest, then he or she must be allowed to the opportunity to pursue topics therein to unlimited levels of inquiry...' When their investigation is completed they can 'revolve' out of the programme until they are ready to undertake another one.

As with many strategies for working with gifted and talented pupils the emphasis is on flexibility. Speaking at a conference at

Brunel University in June 2004, Renzulli stated that one of the golden rules of his enrichment method was that '...the normal rules of schooling are suspended...'

Ian Warwick

Ian is Development Director for London Gifted and Talented, a consortium that supports the capital's schools. Ian is a practising teacher with 18 years experience in Inner London comprehensives and has spent 7 years working in gifted and talented provision. He is an interesting speaker on areas such as online provision and building independent learning and his presentation shows how the London Gifted and Talented models apply to personalised learning in these fields.

Joan Freeman

Joan is a very influential writer and researcher in the field of gifted and talented education. Her work includes the effects of gender and why bright girls underachieve in post-school life despite examination success that equals that of boys. She has now published the very readable Gifted Children Grown Up (Freeman, 2001), which follows a group of 210 recognised and unrecognised gifted children over 25 years, describing what happened to them and to their families. Based on earlier research she has also produced a useful checklist for very able pupils (*Box 3.1*):

Box 3.1 Research-based check list for very able pupils

- **Memory and knowledge** – excellent memory and use of information.

- **Self-regulation** – they know how they learn best and can monitor their learning.

- **Speed of thought** – they may spend longer on planning but then reach decisions more speedily.

- **Dealing with problems** – they add to information, spot what is irrelevant and get to the essentials more quickly.

- **Flexibility** – although their thinking is usually more organised than other children's, they can see and adopt alternative solutions to learning and problem solving.

- **Preference for complexity** – they tend to make games and tasks more complex to increase interest.

- **Concentration** – they have exceptional ability to concentrate at will and for long periods of time from an early age.

- **Early symbolic ability** – they may speak, read and write very early.

CONTINUING PROFESSIONAL DEVELOPMENT

In such a recent area as gifted and talented education it is essential that you keep up to date with what is happening. Attendance at conferences and courses, although not mandatory, will help you keep up with the changes in a rapidly expanding field:

Conferences

The DfES now run a termly standing conference that brings together pupils, parents, governors, schools, higher education and research, gifted and talented organisations, and central and local government, in order to provide a forum to advance gifted and talented education. The conference is the responsibility of Gifted and Talented Education Unit (GTEU), which is headed by Tim Dracup who gives delegates updates on recent policy developments. Keynote speakers include people such as Deborah Eyre and there are some excellent workshops. If you're still not sure yourself how creativity can be part of what giftedness means, try to attend one of the workshops given by the Bigfoot Theatre company. Karl Wozny and his colleagues will leave you in no doubt.

Written into the programme of conferences like this is a session entitled 'Networking'. This is an extended coffee break of 45 minutes or so to enable participants to meet and discuss ideas together. Networking generally takes place in an exhibition area where groups such as NACE, the National Primary Trust, and independent groups like Cineclub, the young filmmakers' network, promote their ideas. If you don't know anyone there you can always browse at one of these stands and will very soon find you have the email addresses of half a dozen new people.

The other thing to note about the DfES conferences is that they're free. If you can, get yourself an invitation and your head will only have to pay for the cover. If there is money in the school budget for continuing professional development, however, there are independent companies such as Optimus Publishing and MA Education Ltd who are now organising conferences that feature many of the names already mentioned as speakers and contributors.

Courses

Attendance of an award-bearing course is an excellent way forward in career terms and there are many of these in gifted and talented education which lead to a certificate or diploma, or even as a module of a larger MA course like the one offered by Oxford Brookes at ReCAP, which is fairly typical in style and content.

Such a course will introduce you to the exciting field of action research. This may involve carrying out an audit of your school's current provision for gifted and talented, which can be done by scrutiny of relevant documents such as syllabuses and inspection reports, and by interviewing staff with subject responsibilities. You may be surprised at what you find.

It will also encourage you to carry out research with your own class into how you could raise levels of attainment among a group of identified able children. You might, for instance, wish to raise levels in scientific investigation in a year five class. The course will help you to carry out an 'intervention' and observe and measure the outcome. Techniques for gathering data such as interviewing and observation are taught and practised on the course, tools which you will be able to use with both adults and children as you carry out the research. Ethical considerations for this type of activity are also dealt with clearly. A useful introduction to data gathering techniques is Denscombe's *The Good Research Guide* (1998), an invaluable aid for small-scale research projects.

You may also be asked to disseminate your own learning on the course to your school colleagues. On of the most interesting aspects of the Oxford Brookes course is the nominal group technique. This is a training method in which course participants are asked to share their understanding of what a 'more able' pupil looks like and arrive at consensus. The course members then replicate the session for staff at a training day in

their schools. Asking colleagues how they would define a gifted and talented pupil is a good starting point in the minefield of terminology that both you and they will encounter during your tenure as coordinator.

The course will also include a historical perspective on gifted and talented education. It is useful to know about the previously mentioned *Parliamentary Select Committee Report on Highly Able Children* (House of Commons Education and Employment Committee, 1999). This report is well worth reading and includes useful points such as '...the search for a precise definition (of high ability) might distract schools form finding ways to meet the needs of their most able children...' and '...if we consider children who are in the top 20 per cent as regards to all-round ability or ability in a particular area, one might find that up to 30 to 40 per cent of pupils in a school are included...' a point also made by Deborah Eyre (1997).

Award-bearing courses, however, also include a substantial written element in the form of an assignment sometimes consisting of 4000 words or more. Before you throw up your hands in horror at the prospect of spending hours hunched over the word processor (hours which would be better spent with your family) just consider the advantages. First, it provides intellectual challenge and you must have wanted this or you wouldn't have taken on the role in the first place. Second, it shows that you can do what you expect your pupils to do every day – put yourself on the line to be assessed. Finally, it's a good excuse to get out of doing the Saturday morning shopping!

Joking aside, many LEAs have systems to provide paid study leave for 1 or 2 days to carry out library research and writing the essays, so it's worth finding out in good time whether yours does. In the end, achieving success with an assignment can be tremendously satisfying and do wonders for the self-esteem. That is not to say that passing them is easy – in fact quite the reverse. The tutors have to mark to fairly strict criteria in order to satisfy the demands of the institution and may even ask for the assignment to be resubmitted if it doesn't fulfil the requirements.

Reading

One of the hazards of attending such courses is that you come away with voluminous reading lists to which you are rarely able to do justice. Just because you have 6 weeks' holiday doesn't mean you wouldn't rather spend it curled up with a novel you haven't had the time to read during term-time.

However, if you enjoy reading, there is plenty here to get your teeth into. Apart from the books already mentioned, there are particular publications that are invaluable to coordinators at all levels. One such is *Exploring G&T Transition* by Angela Chapman (2003). In it she discusses the problems that still exist for primary to secondary transfer, and argues how important it is that we 'get it right' for the gifted and talented pupil. She argues that if we don't, it will cause disaffection and underachievement among able pupils resulting in poor behaviour.

A good example is from her section on gifted and talented maths issues. The problem raised is that secondary teachers tended to dismiss claims by primary schools, parents and the pupils themselves that they possess exceptional mathematical ability. Pupils were sent from primary school to advanced maths centres in order to work in a more challenging and stimulating environment. Angela Chapman uses this to highlight the contrast between the levels of support offered by the different phases. At secondary level, she says, this level of support is not always available and this can lead to a change in pupils' attitudes as they progress through the system, resulting in poor performance and results and even in dropping out of the system altogether.

The book contains excellent suggestions on how to manage transition between key stages. Using research by Galton et al (1999), she explains how administrative, social, curriculum, pedagogic and management bridges can be built between the key stages in order to facilitate this. It also includes a wealth of other information such as good practice contact addresses, websites and organisations supporting able children.

Another book that is worth reading is the aforementioned Joan Freeman's *Gifted Children Grown Up* (2001). If you have any doubts about the importance of your role, this book will silence them. She writes with warmth and humour about a study which she began in 1974, and which she carried out over more than 20 years into the developing lives of 210 children identified as 'gifted'. She deals with the successes and failures of these pupils and how we might avoid the latter in the future. It's an absolute page-turner.

Reading will also help you to deal with your colleagues' calls for help with their teaching of the 'bright group'. Get hold of

Barry Teare's (1999) book, *Effective Resources for Able and Talented Children*. It begins with ideas on how to build a curriculum for the more able, but if you just want to offer quick lesson solutions, it contains a fund of ideas on different subject areas. In the section on geography, for example, is an activity called 'On the Map'. This is a demanding activity where pupils construct a map using six-figure grid references to add some fixed points and others that are open to interpretation. There is a photocopiable (a teacher's best friend!) grid template on which the side of each individual square represents one kilometre. There is then a creative element where pupils are asked to add their own features. Possible solutions are offered at the end.

Not only are there good books but there also numerous articles out there about gifted and talented education. *G&T Update*, published by Optimus, is an excellent source. Browsing through back issues you might find out, for instance, about the ideas of the psychologist Mihaly Csikszentmihalyi and colleagues (1997). From the work of artists whom he studied for his postgraduate thesis, he discovered what is called 'flow' – a state in which people are so involved in an activity that nothing else seems to matter. He used the idea of flow in a study he made of 200 able teenagers to discover why some developed their abilities while others gave up. He found that flow was the strongest predictor of how far the student progressed in the schools curriculum with his or her ability.

He and his co-authors also suggest three ways of promoting positive results in the classroom, and these are all ideas worth taking on board by coordinators for passing on to colleagues

- The most influential teachers are those who always continue to nurture their interest in their subjects.
- Everything should be done to minimise the impact of rules, exams and procedures and to focus on the satisfaction of learning.

■ Teachers must read the shifting needs of learners and know when to hold back and when to intervene.

Research

Although this is not easy to set up, if you get the opportunity it is worthwhile doing some of your own research into methods that work in your teaching of gifted and talented pupils. As mentioned before a gifted and talented course may offer you an opportunity to do action research, and many LEAs have their own schemes through which teachers can examine and disseminate their own practice. Bedfordshire for example runs a professional study group system by which teachers in all subject areas present colleagues in their upper, middle and lower school pyramids with ideas they have been using in their teaching.

NAGTY now has a national competition where you can carry out research related to gifted and talented provision. If you are accepted for this, you and your school receive a sum of £5000 to support your research.

You start by submitting a proposal of interest (based on research ideas you have already) to NAGTY for a Developing Expertise Award. If the research team find your proposal of interest, you are invited to attend a training day at Warwick University, where a group of academics such as Dr Wendy Robinson and Professor Jim Campbell guide you towards a more detailed proposal for your research. You are also introduced to other applicants with whom you discuss and share your ideas.

The tough part is that at the end you have to go away and write about your proposal in some depth. If you can show the team that you have refined a research question and can collect qualitative or quantitative data on this, which will develop the quality of teaching and learning for gifted and talented pupils in your school, the award will be granted. As it is a competition, however, only ten out of the 20 proposals submitted will be accepted, so the whole process does require a great deal of commitment.

If you should find that attending courses and carrying out research has reawakened writing skills that you had forgotten about then publications like the NACE Newsletter *Teaching and Learning*, and *G&T Update* will often accept articles that you have written about your practice. Editors are friendly and approachable and some of them will even pay you for your piece.

Websites

All major figures and groups mentioned in this book have websites attached to them, which are generally easy to find and navigate. There are many useful sites which are listed at the end of this book but one which you will probably find invaluable is the website for NAGTY, www.nagty.ac.uk.

NAGTY was established by the government in 2002 and is now directed by Deborah Eyre. Among its aims is a mission to ensure that all gifted and talented children in England can maximise their potential, to ensure that all members of the education profession have the knowledge and skills to meet these pupils' needs, and to become the leading world centre for research and development in the field. The site deals with four areas of NAGTY:

- Expertise Centre – links teachers to relevant knowledge and expertise.
- Student Academy – gives members access to short courses, summer schools academic study groups and online forums.
- Professional Academy – works with schools to ensure that every teacher feels confident in catering for gifted pupils in their class.
- Research Centre – contributes to CPD by, among other things, organising school-based research.

Handy Hints

- There are a number of well-known names in gifted and talented education.
- Continuing professional development in the form of courses and conferences is vital to help you keep up to date with developments in the field.
- Keep reading around the subject – you may find new ways of doing things.
- Undertaking research involving your pupils can help develop your career and is likely to interest the pupils as well.

CHAPTER 4

ACHIEVING TARGETS AND STRATEGY GOALS

What are your targets and how do you achieve them? First of all you need to establish general principles for your school such as:

- Gifted and talented is a whole school issue.
- Excellence is expected – it's cool to be clever.
- Gifted and talented provision needs to be monitored continuously at all levels.

The 'whole school' issue is an important one and can be introduced with messages like 'a rising tide lifts all ships'. There is evidence to support the idea that if you raise the standards of the more able it will improve those of everybody else and you may well have found this true in your own teaching experience. For it to be a 'whole school' issue it needs to be led from the top and supported by senior management. It then has to be kept in the forefront of people's minds by you, the coordinator, until ideally you could leave the school for your next job, leaving behind a structure that would continue to operate without you.

Of course, we all know that life in busy schools doesn't often work like that and another way that you can stamp the idea on the school is to make it 'okay to be clever'. Having a general expectation of excellence in the classroom and celebrating achievement is the preferred way but it is not always enough. Surprisingly, many children find that it's not okay to be clever and go to great lengths to hide their abilities. In the world of the classroom, the dread of being called a 'boffin' runs deep and the school must do what it can to challenge that perception. One school persuaded one of its most difficult pupils to attend an out-of-hours drama course where he could use his prodigious talent for improvisation in a positive way. Although he still spent much time in isolation, the school had recognised that he was not entirely a lost cause and he could celebrate some success among his peers.

Provision for gifted and talented continually needs be looked at afresh. Policies have a habit of gathering dust and becoming 'just-another-thing-that-I-must-get-round-to-looking-at!'. Also, if a policy has been in operation for a while, it is possible that the staff profile may have changed. In one school after 5 years of gifted and talented provision there were only half the subject coordinators left who were there when the programme began. Getting colleagues involved in writing and implementing the policy is a way of creating ownership and finding out what is required.

Once you are clear about general principles you can get down to specific targets that you want to achieve. Ask yourself what is going to happen that didn't happen before? There are a number of things you can aim at but your priorities should be:

- staff training
- having a policy
- identifying and tracking progress of pupils
- working successfully with parents
- liaising with transfer schools.

STAFF TRAINING

Training staff is crucial to your success as a coordinator. Gifted and talented provision is just one more initiative in a sea of many things that colleagues have to accommodate in their teaching. It is useful here to share training ideas with other coordinators and even ask those who have carried out successful training days in their own schools to come and talk at yours, possibly on a day set aside for whole staff development.

As mentioned before, using a nominal group technique is a good training method if the concept of gifted and talented is a relatively new one to staff. This method, based on the Oxford Brookes University (2001) guidelines, ensures that everyone contributes, allows a wide variety of responses and avoids the dominance of the group by a few people with strong ideas.

Nominal group techniques

1. **Task presentation**
   The task is written up to be visible to everyone, e.g. what is your definition of an able pupil?, or how would you identify an able pupil?

2. **Task clarification**
   A shared understanding of the question is essential. Ensure that everyone involved understands the nature of the task they are undertaking.

3. **Silent nomination**
   Everyone lists a private response to the question (10 minutes).

4. **Personal ranking**
   Individuals then rank their own list to establish what they feel are priorities.

5. **Master list**
   The leader (you) then compiles a master list for all to see taking one item from each group member in turn. No editing of material or evaluative comments should be made at this stage.

6. **Item clarification**

    Each item is discussed until all members know what it means. If a member of the group feels that their item is already covered they may request its withdrawal.

    No pressure should be applied to any individual to have items withdrawn or incorporated in another.

7. **Evaluation**

    The group should now decide the relative importance of each item. Each person is allowed five weighted votes, five for the point that is felt to be the most important, four for the next etc. A simple voting procedure will now allow a consensus to emerge.

8. **Discussion**

    Now that a group picture has emerged, more general discussion can proceed.

As the leader of the session keep these things in mind:

- Do not reinterpret a person's ideas.
- Use the participant's own wording.
- Do not interject your own ideas – you are not participating.
- Give people time to think.
- This is not a debate – do not allow participants to challenge each other or attempt to persuade each other.
- Do not try to interpret results – do not look for patterns.

You will probably find that it's easier than it looks, but if you can manage all this successfully you are well on the way to becoming a good gifted and talented coordinator. If some commitment to gifted and talented provision is already in place among your staff, then a more specific training session may be required as they begin to want to include provision for gifted and talented pupils in their lesson. One way is to use a model of BS Bloom's higher order thinking (1956). This, according to Deborah Eyre, '...has a clear structure to enable planning and can be adapted to a wide variety of subject areas.' In *Able Children in Ordinary Schools* (1997), Eyre shows a diagram of the building blocks showing high, middle and lower order thinking skills. She then gives a series of examples of lessons drawn from work with primary teachers in Oxfordshire.

One headteacher in Bedfordshire used Bloom's method (1956) on a training day by forming the staff into random groups and giving out a resource to each group. The resources were artefacts, which she had collected from various departments; musical instruments, PE equipment, a tenon saw, a map of the world and an ornamental paperweight from home. Her idea was to address a variety of subject areas and get the staff to use the artefacts to plan questions for low, middle and high ability pupils. This resulted in approximately 30 minutes of animated discussion. The staff then moved into subject groups and discussed in their own departments how to put Bloom's model into practice.

Subject departments were then asked by the head to work together on a subsequent training day to create resources for gifted and talented pupils. This was very successful. The art department, for instance, identified a list of skills that the more able would be able to demonstrate such as, 'show a passionate interest in the world of art and design'. This interest could be related to a particular art form, to contemporary culture or youth culture. A range of tasks was then suggested that pupils could carry out to reflect this. One was 'to design a CD cover for a new musical group with reference to artists whose work was pertinent to the subject'.

The English department came up with an exciting idea – a 'Carpe Diem' club, which would meet once a month after school and

would involve a mixed group of selected pupils from years seven and eight. They would tackle novels like Michael Morpurgo's *Kensuke's Kingdom* and visit a local theatre for a Shakespeare 4 Kidz performance of *Romeo and Juliet*.

Although the headteacher was gratified by the results of the training, she now has to deal with numerous requests for funding. Unless you are part of a grant-funded programme like Excellence in Cities, there is no specific money for gifted and talented education. She has set aside part of the budget and has asked teachers in subject departments to bid for sums to cover what they wish to do for the gifted and talented, over and above their normal allowance.

GIFTED AND TALENTED POLICY

Writing your own policy will really let you get your mind around the ideas you are presenting to other people on the staff. It will also let them know that you are serious. It's a good idea to look at other school policies before you begin but if you can't get hold of any, Eyre has an excellent example in her book *Able Children in Ordinary Schools* (1997) as do NAGC (National Association for Gifted Children) and ReCAP. Most coordinators, however, will be only too pleased to let you share the fruits of their hard work

If you can get colleagues involved in writing the policy, then so much the better. It will give them some ownership and help you to find out what is required. One way to achieve this is to give out a staff questionnaire. Unlike the bank questionnaires that none of us ever fill in, it is easy to get them back because you are likely to see your colleagues face to face each day. The question 'have you managed to complete that questionnaire yet?' is likely to be met with a profuse apology and a promise to deliver it the very next day!

Once the policy is in place, use it to move gifted and talented education forward. The first thing you will probably have to do is present it to the school governors. They are likely to be impressed, but slightly mystified as to why the school hasn't been doing it all before. Here's where your diplomatic skills have to come into play. Tell them that up to 30 per cent of the school could be regarded as gifted and talented and that five per cent will have exceptional ability. But don't give hostages to fortune. You may have to explain to them that the process implementing the strategy will be a gradual one, owing to all the other initiatives already in the pipeline of any school.

Identifying pupils

The target of identifying pupils is very likely to be the most difficult for the reasons already explained. Remember that it is not just your responsibility to make the identification, but also that of the colleagues who teach pupils in the classroom. Methods of organising the identification of pupils will vary from school to school. In one primary school, classroom teachers were asked to identify their individual pupils on a 'hard' and a 'soft' list, in other words, those whose overall performance gave certainty would be on the former, while those for whom the teacher needed further evidence would be on the latter.

In a large middle school of 750 pupils this is what happened – first, each head of subject was asked to provide the coordinator with a list of ten per cent of the most able pupils in their subject in each year group. To do this, the subject coordinator first had to ask individual teachers to provide her with names and pass these on to the gifted and talented coordinator. The coordinator then collated the resulting lists first by subject and then alphabetically by year group. Copies of these lists were placed in the staff room and given to both year and subject heads. Teachers and other staff were also asked to notify the coordinator if any further changes needed to be made.

Having provision in place

You have to make sure, however, that identification of pupils does not become an end in itself. It only has value if it leads to better provision for those who have been identified. On the plus side, it should be easy to see from these lists which pupils have a talent in one specific area and which possess ability across the board. You now have to ensure that 'something else' is happening in classrooms to meet their needs. It is that something else which, after the process of identification, will create the biggest problem for teachers.

The question that faces the teacher is this: What do I have to do differently to cater for these pupils? Unlike those on the school's SEN register, gifted and talented pupils do not have statutory support, nor is there a long tradition of dealing with their needs as there is for the teaching of the less able. There are, however, a number of strategies that a school can employ.

STRATEGIES

Setting

In larger schools setting is often decided upon as the simplest option. It is easy to organise and generally satisfies parental expectations. On the downside it can create elitism among pupils in the top sets and a consequent feeling of worthlessness in those of the lower ones. This can also even extend to the teachers of those pupils.

Movement between sets is often difficult to manage especially if the setting criteria in the first place are too narrow. In English, for example, year seven might be set on the basis of year six SATs test results but this means that there is a great deal of ability in English that has been ignored. Drama, for instance is a key area where gifts and talents for language and expression in English can be developed and yet it does not feature strongly in the National Curriculum. Despite these arguments, however, teachers often prefer setting to mixed ability teaching as the planning and organisation is less onerous.

Many teachers acknowledge maths as a subject where 'setting' is needed beyond year six but the verdict on subjects like science and even French is less clear. Mixed ability teaching can be used in both these subjects but to be effective there has to be a different classroom approach and lessons will need to be far less teacher-led and favour a greater reliance on independent learning.

Independent learning

Independent learning is, of course, the kind of learning that you want to lead if you are going to make a success of your gifted and talented policy. In order to enable pupils to become independent learners, it is important that teachers learn to relinquish control over what happens in the classroom. Having the confidence to allow pupils to have this control is another matter. Teachers are working in a largely proscribed curriculum where the scope to be different is somewhat restricted.

In addition, independent learning is great in theory but notoriously difficult to put into practice. Events at William Tyndale School in Islington in the 1970s will underline this point (Ellis et al, 1977).

In 1971, in the Black papers, two academics, Brian Cox and AE Dyson, had begun the backlash against standards and behaviour in the comprehensives. 'Child-centred education' was an emerging issue in the media and the papers were full of stories from William Tyndale, where the headteacher ran the school as a cooperative and told a governor he 'did not give a damn about parents'.

To be successful, independent learning has to be strongly led and supported by a staff committed to taking risks and trying out new ideas.

A good example of where independent learning is working is at St John's School in Marlborough, Wiltshire. For a third of the pupils in year seven, volunteer staff have written and facilitated a thematic curriculum where pupils work in pairs or small groups asking and answering their own questions about areas like 'making the news', 'forests' and 'what makes us unique'. Two years after its inception the idea is still flourishing there and at a number of other schools who are trying out the ideas. The project is called Opening Minds and was the inspiration of the Royal Society of Arts. Pupils taking part in both the top and bottom of the range showed a marked improvement in achievement and behaviour.

In my own experience, a number of opportunities for independent learning can occur within the confines of the key stage 2 science curriculum.

I used an idea, taken from the Qualifications and Curriculum Authority (QCA) (2000) document Raising Standards *that pupils should be asked to design and make a burglar alarm that would work if a burglar accidentally set it off. Circuits and switch designs had already been taught, as had the use of diagrams. The pupils were asked to draw an initial plan, make the alarm and then record the experiment using circuit diagrams. Daniel was a keen and able scientist who had great difficulty with writing anything down. With the drawing, practical and diagram format, however, he was in his element. His original design includes two LEDs [light-emitting diodes] and a buzzer. He had to experiment and work out how to use a parallel circuit in order for all the components to operate. This he achieved and for his recording I taught him how to use a diagram of a parallel circuit. Daniel went on to achieve a good level 5 in his science SAT at key stage 2.*

The third element of Renzulli and Rees's (1985) triad (average ability, task commitment and creativity interact) – creativity – was never more appropriate than now. Independent learning

is necessarily creative in that it requires initiative in order for the pupil to choose his or her own routes through the learning terrain. Learning styles have a big part to play here. Most pupils (even if they haven't been able to express it) have a preferred learning style. Unsurprisingly, this rarely involves listening to the teacher for very long. Literacy consultant Alan Peat, while talking about raising writing results at a conference in Bedford, famously said that '...concentration span is chronological age plus one minute'. In other word theirs is much less than yours, however able they might appear to be.

If colleagues are still not convinced, another way forward way forward on the subject of independent learning is to ask the pupils themselves. A report, *It's Like Mixing Colours*, by Eileen Carnell (2004) of the Institute of Education shows that among other things, young people want the following:

- To be trusted more and given more responsibility for their learning.

- Fewer pointless tests that interfere with their learning.
- To be listened to and have their views acted upon.

From her research Eileen Carnell found that when a less controlling approach was used with pupils in the classroom, they were able to succeed on their own terms.

Traditional

There is still leaves scope for a more traditional approach. For instance, in a mixed ability religious education lesson in one primary school, teachers use three sets of worksheets for the lower, middle and higher ability range. Pupils are grouped according to reading ability and work at their own level with support from the teacher and a Learning Support Assistant.

Whatever is claimed in the press about traditionalists versus progressives, most schools' teaching force is made up of a well-balanced mixture of both and it is your role as coordinator to take everyone along with you. Teachers are busy people and haven't a lot of time to juggle ideas, however brilliant they may appear in principle.

Tracking pupils

Once your identification and teaching procedures are in place, you will need to track pupils to see if the policy is working for them at each stage of their school career. This is best attempted when the policy has been in place for two or three years. Following the progress of one pupil in a Bedfordshire Middle School is a way of illustrating the benefits of this process for the coordinator.

When Stacie started the school in year five her parents, who had been told by the lower school that she was bright, were concerned about her lack of substantial achievement. These concerns were presented to her form teacher and year head at the end of year five and the beginning of year six but had assumed only a nuisance value and were talked away at parents' evenings. By the end of year six, despite achieving level 5 in all three subjects, Stacie was only officially identified as gifted and talented in history. This continued through years seven and eight with just a single entry under history and yet it was clear to the gifted and talented coordinator that this girl had considerable gifts, especially in the area of self-presentation at which she was adept.

Knowing that Stacie's parents would be supportive, the coordinator enrolled her on a weekend course run by the Frontiers Club for key stage 3 pupils on a Saturday. This was an out-of-hours learning facility run by Bedfordshire County Council to offer able pupils opportunities that they could not receive at their schools. The course was entitled 'Creative Performance' and showed Stacie, who had a tendency towards precocity, how to present herself to others in a more mature and understated way.

Eventually the coordinator decided to use this ability to give Stacie appropriate recognition in the school. She knew from talking to her that Stacie was skilled at giving PowerPoint presentations and so she asked her to give one to year six who would be eligible for the Frontiers Club the following year. With some help and support from friends, Stacie spoke knowledgeably and enthusiastically about the variety of courses at the Frontiers Club.

Parents

Stacie's case study shows how by monitoring individual progress using the lists pupils can be directed in to a more appropriate channel for their abilities. It also indicates how important it is for the coordinator to have the confidence of both pupils and parents. It is important to work alongside parents and involve them as much as possible in the processes, if results are to be positive. The jury is still out in staff rooms on how much you should tell parents about whether or not their child is able; it is always best to be as open and upfront as possible about what you are trying to do. As already mentioned, if you have a good policy in place, train your staff, and identify pupils, there is no reason why parents should not be satisfied with the provision that the school is making for their child.

Transition and transfer – links between schools

Unless you get this right, a great deal of your efforts will be wasted in the future. Angela Chapman's (2003) study *Exploring G&T Transition* points to the fact that traditionally communication between primary and secondary schools has been poor and that on the gifted and talented issues, the stimulating and challenging environment provided at primary school often did not continue into the secondary phase. Many secondary schools now have regular subject liaison meetings with feeder primary schools; you cannot be expected to attend them all however many hats you wear, so you should ensure that gifted and talented issues are a regular agenda item.

> *Sarah, who had been identified as very able in every academic subject area in her middle school, was due to transfer at age 13. Fortunately, a very proactive coordinator for gifted and talented pupils at the upper school had organised liaison meetings during which information on pupils like Sarah had been shared. This coordinator had organised an excellent enrichment activities programme in the school. Students in the year nine intake, who had been identified as gifted and talented in three subject areas or less, were invited to join any activities on the enrichment programme.*

The enrichment activities programme included science, language and art 'master classes', 'maths challenge' competitions and even a film club.

Those like Sarah, who had been identified in four or more subject areas, would have in addition an Individual Learning Plan (ILP) and also an interview with the coordinator and the careers advisor. They would also have school support for applying to the National Academy for Gifted and Talented Youth (NAGTY). Owing to the good communication between coordinators, Sarah is in line to follow this programme.

Handy Hints

- Make sure you have general principles in place within your school for teaching gifted and talented pupils.
- Staff training is vital for full implementation of any programme.
- The policy itself should be clear and prominent.
- Input of all teachers is important for identification of pupils and provision for pupils.
- Ensure you have strategies for putting provision in place
- A policy for transition and transfer to other schools is also vital.

CHAPTER 5

THE TEACHING ROOM

YOUR 'STAGE'

Rooms send out messages to pupils about what is expected from them. If the desks are set out in rows it is likely that the teacher will be directing operations from the front and the learning style will be one of listening and taking in information. If, on the other hand, the desks are in pairs forming tables, then the learning style will be more interactive.

As the gifted and talented coordinator you may have a clear idea about which arrangement is most suitable for gifted and talented pupils but you can only advise about classroom design, not dictate. For some curriculum areas like science or PE it may be simple, as the teacher will have a specialist room such as a laboratory or gymnasium to operate in; for others such as English, room design which favours the gifted and talented pupil can be far more challenging.

In many ways, the teacher is like an actor and the classroom is the stage. The difference is that you are also the director and you can make the stage how you want it to be to suit your teaching style for the play you are about to create. For the teaching of a diverse and exciting English curriculum to able pupils, the room should be flexible. It might have to be a newspaper office, a forum for group discussion, a drama studio or a lecture theatre. An example from my own experience will illustrate this.

The classroom, designed with the help of my 16-year-old daughter, was to suit the teaching and learning of an able year seven English group with whom I was researching the effect of collaborative group work. The room was large and had two main doors, one opening out onto a grassed and tree-scattered area and the other leading into a computer room. There were sixteen desks to seat a maximum of 32 pupils. As the room was also used for maths and geography, where the teaching style was more instructive, I had to be able to transform it quickly from an instruction room to one where there would be seven sets of four tables for working in groups. Together we decided to create a mixture of paired desks and single desks so that this could take place and although there were some grumbles from more traditional colleagues who used the room, the arrangement has remained in place ever since.

I always used the instructive mode to give directions as to how the lessons were to proceed. On the non-interactive whiteboard, I wrote down in advance what had to be covered in the lesson, giving approximate times for completion of each section. When the pupils entered for the start of a poetry lesson the board might read:

- *What is a poem? Make an ideas map individually (10 min).*

- *In groups share quotations about poetry from book page nine (15 min).*

- *Discuss ideas in groups and write a shared paragraph about poetry (25 min).*

- *Read out paragraphs to the class (10 min).*

Pupils would already have been shown how to take roles for group work such as chair, scribe, collector and checker so the lesson would proceed as planned with me circulating round the tables. Sometimes I would ask one of the pupils to video the lesson, focusing on the group processes as they worked. The emphasis was on flexibility, and movement around the classroom was relaxed when pupils wanted to collect materials, ask questions of me or to take on water.

Sometimes an envoy method was used where one member of each group would take the ideas of his/her group to share with another.

The book we used was the excellent The Poetry Book *published by the English and Media Centre (Bleiman et al, 2001). At the end of the series of poetry lessons using the book the board read as follows:*

- *Instructions for presenting poems (10 min).*

- *Discuss methods of presenting chosen poem (10 min).*

- *Plan and practise presentation (20 min).*

- *Give presentation – this will be videoed (20 min).*

- *Write an evaluation of your performance for homework.*

For part of this lesson the room was a workshop and then became a drama studio during the presentations. Chairs and tables had to be pushed back for space and this often caused a break in the lessons. With some persuasion from the pupils I eventually realised that if the weather was fine it would be far better to spill outside onto the grass and give the presentations beneath the trees: a miniature Forest of Arden!

The role-playing was important and, as the group became more familiar with the idea, the room became an editorial office where a school newsletter called R U Up 4 It? was produced. As the room was adjacent to the computer room, the use of the school laptops was easily arranged and writing short pieces to order was developed on these. I really began to look forward to these lessons as they were pushing forward my own skills as a teacher

'Can we have more lessons like this?', asks Jonathan, who with a group of pupils had just produced a television broadcast about Skellig, *a book by David Almond (1998), which the class had been reading. Here is part of the script for the broadcast:*

Miguel: Hello, and welcome to today's programme. Today we will be welcoming Amanda Driver and a group of actors who will help us recreate a few scenes from Skellig, *our book of the week. So, Amanda, can you give me a briefing of the book?*

Amanda: Well, what happens is Michael is the main character and he finds a man in his garage called Skellig?

Miguel: Does anyone else know about Skellig?

Amanda: A girl called Mina who is going out with Michael.

Miguel: What is your favourite bit of the book?

Amanda: When Michael and Mina discover Skellig *is an angel.*

Miguel: What is the most exciting part of the book?

Amanda: When the baby nearly dies so you want to read on.

Miguel: Do you think the writer should write any more Skellig *books?*

Amanda: There probably wouldn't be any more to write about.

Miguel: Could Skellig *be made into a film do you think*

Amanda: Yes, here is a little part of what the film might look like.

[Amanda, Emma and Jonathan enact part of the story]

Amanda: So what do you think of that piece of acting?

Miguel: It was quite good

Amanda: Do you think it matched the book?

Miguel: It did quite a bit.

[They enact another part]

Miguel: Well, thank you for coming Amanda and showing us that fabulous piece of acting.

Amanda: No problem. It was a pleasure.

Miguel: Well goodbye to our viewers at home and goodnight. If you have any further questions about the film, Skellig, *click on our website and talk to Amanda herself.*

From comments such as Jonathan's, the creative work displayed and from the results of independent observation and interview which researchers carried out for me, I knew that the approach was working. (Leyland, 2003)

Reflections

This example is specific to one teacher and subject and in that sense is quite narrow. What it illustrates is that the teacher can adapt his/her environment to suit the needs of the more able child. Renzulli and Rees (1985) said that '...enrichment activities, which met pupils' particular interests, could take place in the regular classroom, in a special resource room, in an independent study group in the library or even in the community.'

It is surprising just how little attention has been given to classroom design and, of course, no one ever seems to ask the pupils what they think. In a very interesting book called *The School I'd Like*, by Catherine Burke and Ian Grosvenor (2003), however, pupils were able to put forward their views about classrooms.

> *'The activity room would be a place to go after your work is finished. There will be several activities such as painting, an IT area, a reading area, a communication area, a music area and a sensory room to inspire good thoughts. The communication area is a place where you can talk to people all over the world by just putting on some headphones and a microphone...the machine will translate any other languages.'* Sophie, 10

Another pupil spoke of the importance of computer technology:

> *'Instead of having to hand write lots of notes during lessons which is time consuming and boring for both pupils and teachers, information packs would be written on the computer to cover every subject in the curriculum as well as assignments. These packs would be accessible through the internet as well so members of the school could view them at home as well as at school.'* Alice, 13

Or even:

> *'In my perfect school there would be no square classrooms but instead, triangular ones so that no one could sulk in the back row.'* Sam, 14

In an article in the *Observer* newspaper there was a report about how the Design Council has set up a project relating to the flexible classroom. One school, St Margaret's in Aigburth, Liverpool is the place for one of these classrooms. Interestingly enough, St Margaret's was built on a site that originally consisted of Taylor's Farm and Bluebell Wood and is about half a mile from the River Mersey, a heritage that seems oddly appropriate for the classroom of the future.

> *'...The classroom is circular and rotates through 360 degrees. The teacher, instead of standing at the front, circles the pupils on a*

curved racetrack and can also take up a position on a podium in the middle. The pupils sit at Q-Pods, which are special table and chair units on wheels. These can easily moved to different positions in the room when group work is required. The pupils work with marker pens on large whiteboards which are removed and replaced on the walls of the room so the classes' work can be discussed. The temperature and light in the room is electronically controlled and the boards can also act as screens for computer projections. One pupil, impressed by the idea said, 'In a normal classroom they cram everything on one board and you can't see it.' Another said, 'It is also much more fun. We get the boards down all the time and work together – before we would work more on our own in maths. This has made maths much more fun than it used to be...' (Thorpe and Asthana, 2005).

Although not specifically an idea to meet the needs of gifted and talented pupils, this flexible and creative approach to classroom design is one that will suit them as the case study showed. In an age of interactive whiteboards and where pupils can call up a PowerPoint presentation for homework at the touch of a button, the need for both these methods of classroom design is easy to see.

Handy Hints

- The classroom is your stage – make sure it works to your full advantage.
- Pupils' views on ideal classrooms have been researched – you could involve your pupils in arranging your own classroom.
- The classroom of the future may be very different to the one we are used to now.

CHAPTER 6

WORKING WITH COLLEAGUES AND PARENTS OR CARERS

Working successfully with colleagues and parents or carers is clearly going to be one of the key areas of your role and also one of its challenges. Let's start with your colleagues.

COLLEAGUES

As stated before, gifted and talented provision is simply another issue for colleagues to deal with, and it is important that you have their support as well as that of the head in your attempts to put provision on the map in your school. You may well get some positive initial responses such as the comment that, 'It's time we did for the bright ones what we have been doing for the weak children for so long', but that is essentially a negative statement. In order to stress the positive side of gifted and talented provision, you need to create a positive school ethos in which achievement is accepted and acknowledged and where such pupils are praised. As mentioned earlier, it's cool to be clever.

Teachers need to provide support for pupils who fall into the category of able learners in whatever field, as they often lack confidence because of the high standards they set themselves. Teachers who use their own interests in the subject to lead learning can act as good role models for such children to follow. The coordinator of art at a large middle school in Bedfordshire took interested pupils from all years on a series of visits to the Tate Gallery in London. This culminated in a visit of 15 year eight pupils to the Frida Kahlo exhibition. These 'out-of-school trips' were followed by a huge amount of interest in art on the part of the pupils, and a request to the gifted and talented coordinator for the funds to start a lunchtime club in which those pupils could further develop their artistic talents.

Talents

It is often the talent side of the gifted and talented equation that colleagues find difficult to address. Although much has been made of the academic side or 'giftedness', talent in PE, art and music, especially in small schools, may lack the resource of specialist-trained teachers in these fields. Very often pupils may have developed skills and performance, which it is difficult to provide for in the ordinary classroom. You may have to tread carefully here, as colleagues will not be pleased if they feel you are questioning their ability to provide for those talents. Tactful discussion about forming links with the community and with other schools with more specialist facilities will be needed.

For secondary schools the DfES (2004) *KS3 National Strategy* gives a list of approaches for teaching able and gifted and talented pupils, which characterise how successful departments deal with the three talent domains. Beside the more widely known ones of participation in local and national competitions and in extracurricular learning opportunities, there are other useful suggestions:

- Having teachers with a history of and interest in their own practice and performance.
- Strong links with and exploitation of the local community and business resources, and contact with experts in the field beyond school.
- Fostering an awareness of a wide range of career opportunities beyond the school.

One enterprising headteacher of a Bedfordshire lower school had a non-teaching friend who never stopped boasting to her about his mountaineering exploits and the book he was going to write about them. At her school, years one to four were doing a project on air and she wanted raise its profile among colleagues so, taking him at his word, she asked him to give the school an assembly on climbing, showing ropes and crampons and describing the difficulty of breathing normally at high altitude. She even got him to reproduce extracts from the journal and photographs of the equipment to be displayed at the front of the room. When he gave the talk he was surprised at the enormous interest generated among those excited faces, because for him it was a fairly routine experience in which he enjoyed using his talents. We might wonder whether any of those children ever took up the sport for themselves.

Challenge and change

To turn back to the question of giftedness and how colleagues can deal with this in the classroom, David Hargreaves (2004), author of *Working Laterally: How Innovation Networks Make an Education Epidemic*, says that the best way to spread new practices is on a peer to peer basis and that innovations are caught from personal contact (2004). MacGilchrist et al (2004) in *The Intelligent School* suggests that school staff can learn from each other and that if they are also involved in the action research process they are more likely to carry out change. A teacher of French who had experimented with collaborative group work in her year seven mixed ability class reported an improvement in the motivation of able but disaffected boys.

Change, as Francis Duffy (2003) suggests in 'I Think Therefore I am Resistant to Change' in the *Journal of National Staff Development Council*, rests on one's ability to unlearn mental models and 'act outside the box'. The unlearning of these mental models, he says is the key to moving schools forward. Many teachers have a real problem with the concept of giftedness and see it as something very fixed and limited to only a small number of pupils. You, as the coordinator, will have to keep putting before them statements such as Eyre's (1997) that '...around 40 per cent of the cohort of an average comprehensive school are likely to have been identified as able in something or other (where able means being in the top ten per cent of the cohort for that subject)...'.

The challenge is to move colleagues away from a perception that intelligence is fixed and immutable. MacGilchrist et al (2004) discuss the nature of intelligence and of the belief in our culture that it is 'a fixed commodity'. They say that research shows it can be increased through experiences that cultivate metacognition or 'thinking about thinking'. They further argue that pupils tend to live up to the expectations we have of them, and most teachers would endorse this view from their own experience.

If those teachers are on 'the rising tide that lifts all ships' mentioned previously, pupils will benefit. Joan Freeman (2001) argues in *Gifted Children Grow Up* that an enriched curriculum should be a natural part of the school day for all children. 'It can take the form of school outings, experts coming in to school to teach, laboratories left open at the weekend for keen physicists... and many more'.

I have found that having researched methods of raising achievement among able pupils, I was able to apply these methods successfully to those who had been diagnosed as having more moderate ability, giving them a much richer learning experience as a result.

This was a comment from Craig, a pupil identified as being of middle ability, on a poem he had read. The poem was Childhood by Frances Cornford:

> *'We had to read a poem and you could act or do a puppet show. I acted and Jason and Kerry read the poem. I think we did better in our final performance than in our practices...the poem is about a boy who thinks grown-ups want to have stiff backs and wrinkles and at the end he says, "as she was helplessly old and I was helplessly young". I think he was happy that he was young.'*

Educational change

It is worth looking briefly at the recent history of educational change to see if any lessons can be learned there. When the national curriculum was introduced in the late 1980s many primary teachers suddenly had to confront the fact that they had to teach science, despite having had no training and, in some cases, not even having studied it at school. Pockets of excellent primary science practice were in place at the time and many training courses drew on this as they strove to remedy this deficit for numbers of these teachers. I remember working in a number of primary schools in Luton, encouraging pupils and their teachers to be enthusiastic about science. The following is an example of where it worked:

> Susan had been appointed science coordinator the previous year. She was very keen on primary science and was an effective teacher in her own class. She realised, however, that many of her colleagues had a traditional 'teach the basics' approach to the junior school curriculum. They felt that Science was an intrusion and were ill-prepared to teach it. What they found particularly difficult was the active, problem-solving style of teaching required to teach the scientific process skills of Sc1 (Scientific Enquiry strand in the National Curriculum for Science).

> Susan and I decided to run a joint INSET to promote a hands-on approach to science teaching with an emphasis on investigation and problem solving. This took place on the morning of one of the school's closure days. I gave the staff an introduction to the idea of scientific investigation while Susan organised the practical sessions and the report back, which followed them. She had planned sessions on areas such as electricity, bridge building and dissolving, all of which had a highly practical element.

> The morning proceeded in a lively fashion with even the most sceptical staff participating in the activities. As expected, at the end of the morning's activities the feedback that Susan and I received was very positive and left us feeling that we had got our message across. The next problem – would they be able to carry out this kind of teaching activity in their own classrooms?

Well, in the end they had to. The successful introduction of the National Curriculum for Science at KS2 is now history and one could argue that the aims of respected researchers in primary science, like Wynne Harlen (1992), have been achieved if not exactly in the way she had envisaged it.

How then, does this compare with the introduction of gifted and talented education?

There is, of course, no statutory provision for it, only a great deal of interest and enthusiasm at different levels of the education system. There have been statements by ministers such as David Milliband who said, when the incoming Labour government in 1997 announced a radical new emphasis on help and support for gifted and talented children, '...we need to cater for the special needs of every single pupil whether they have a statements of special needs because they are struggling with leaning, or because they have special gifts and talents that mean they are bored in too many lessons and fail to make the most of themselves...'.

Big words indeed and of course, he has already moved on to another area of government, leaving us to make what we will of them. Tony Gardiner of Birmingham University clearly didn't think much of them. In a 2003 article in the TES entitled 'It could be them', he complained that, '...the QCA and the KS3 strategy have generated no strategy through which provision for able mathematicians could be developed...' with the result that in 2003 there were only 55 000 A-level maths candidates, whereas in 1989 there had been 85 000.

The answer to the question is that the introduction of gifted and talented provision will be patchy and it will have to reach a number of compromises as it competes for attention and funding with everything else in education. This is not an argument for giving up. Following a gifted and talented conference, I felt that things weren't going anywhere and asked one of the other delegates for their comments. This was the reply: 'Lots of teachers report similar findings to you but it is changing – just very slowly. I'm afraid it's just a case of chipping away at a block of granite with a pair of blunt nail scissors – very slow progress but your SATs results [the school had achieved 50 per cent level 5 in key stage 2 science] show that progress is happening – honest.'

Changing the angle

- Give the staff a questionnaire (*Box 6.1*) to find out what they think about the gifted and talented policy. I did this when my school's gifted and talented policy had been running for a year. I found that collaborative group work and open-ended tasks were the most common teaching methods used with gifted and talented pupils, although there was a strong feeling that other methods needed to be looked at. The questionnaire revealed that the policy had only moderate impact but that the issue had been raised in teachers' minds and had had some effect on their teaching and organisation. One respondent pointed out the difficulty of altering one's practice in '...a sea of many things'.

- It is likely, however, that colleagues will have to alter their practice in order to be effective in teaching the gifted and talented. In the Excellence in Cities programme, it is recommended that good teaching of gifted and talented pupils, among other things, involves the development of independent learning skills and the ability of the teacher to take risks in order to develop higher levels of thinking. It also says that the teacher needs to be able '...to deploy high level teaching skills in defining expectations, creating a positive classroom climate for enquiry, asking probing questions, managing time and resources, and assessing progress through the lesson...'. (Ofsted, 2001)

- If, despite your enthusiasm about the action research you have carried out, successful training days, your excellent results and the advice from HMI, staff are still not convinced that it relates to their own practice, you might have to change the angle of your approach. Instead of talking about achievement in terms of SATs, talk in terms of the future potential of able pupils and encourage teachers at your school to raise their expectations for all pupils. David Hargreaves (2004) says that like best selling books, innovations have to catch on because '...they are what everybody is excited about'.

Box 6.1
COPY OF STAFF QUESTIONNAIRE

GIFTED AND TALENTED PROVISION/GENDER UNDERACHIEVEMENT:

Questionnaire

The purpose of this questionnaire is firstly to discover how far our gifted and talented policy is succeeding in subject departments throughout the school, and secondly, to discover whether gender underachievement is an issue which needs to be addressed in those subject departments. Results of the questionnaire will be used to advise senior management on both these issues and will be reported on at the next available Heads of Department meeting. Respondents' names will not be disclosed to anyone other than myself. Thank you in advance for your time in completing the questionnaire.

Name:

Dept:

A.   GIFTED AND TALENTED POLICY

Q1.   Do you feel that members of your department are now able to identify gifted and talented children? Please tick

         Yes   No   Don't know

Q2. Are any of the following teaching methods used with able children in your department? Please tick as many as are appropriate and add any comments if you wish:

Setting
Collaborative group work
Mind mapping
Higher order questioning
Open-ended tasks
Differentiated tasks
Thinking skills/problem solving activities
Targeting specific children in the class to do particular tasks
Any other -please specify

Q3. If resources allowed, are there any other strategies you would like to use with gifted and talented children in your subject? E.g. removing small groups to work on separate tasks

Please specify:

Q4. What resource implications would this have? Please tick

LSA support
Money for resources (books etc.)
Any other – please specify

Q5. Have you informed parents that particular children in your subject are able? Please tick

Yes   No

Do you think there is a need for this?

Yes   No

Q6. Are the children that you have identified aware that they are considered able in your subject?

Yes   No

Should they be?

Yes   No

Q7.   How will you monitor whether your department is meeting the
       needs of gifted and talented children? Please tick any relevant
       methods

       Observing identified children
       Looking at their work
       Looking at results of assessments
       Discussion at departmental meetings
       Other – please specify

Q8.   Is there a need for further staff training in:

       i. Identification of gifted and talented children?

       Yes   No

       ii. Methods of teaching gifted and talented children?

       Yes   No

Q9.   Have any forms of external support enabled you to provide for
       able children in your subject, e.g. children's university?
       Please specify

Q10.   Do you think the policy has had any impact on teaching and
       learning at your school? Please tick from 1-5 where 1 is low
       impact and 5 is high.

       1   2   3   4   5

       Please give reasons for your response

B   GENDER UNDERACHIEVEMENT

'It is common to find that high and low ability boys are performing on a par with high and low ability girls – but what about those of average ability? That is often where boys' underachievement can be found. Average girls often go on to get their level 4s at KS2 and their crop of Bs and Cs at GCSE whereas average boys provide the level 3s and the Ds and Es.' (Noble and Bradford, 2000)

This quotation is from research done in Kirklees LEA, where those quoted found that helping underachieving boys also helped the girls.
'Getting it right for boys...and girls' is the title of their book.

1.   Do you think boys, or girls, underachieve in your subject? Please tick

      Boys: Yes   No   Don't know

      Girls: Yes   No   Don't know

Please add any comments to this section:

2.   If this is the case, can you think of any reasons for it? Please specify

3.   If this is an issue that concerns you as a head of department, how do you think it could best be addressed? Please tick any relevant method

Further staff training (please outline type and approach)

Departmental discussion

Whole staff discussion

Other – please specify

Thank you again for responding to this questionnaire

Parents and carers

Parents and carers will be pleased that the school is taking this kind of interest in their child but may not know exactly what it means. You should be able to refer them to the policy and be aware of what their child's achievement has been in previous schools. It is important here that your school liaison policy is working. It would be embarrassing for you to discover half way through the year that the pupil now languishing in lower set English had won a national poetry competition at his previous school. Parents and carers have a big stake in gifted and talented provision and so good communication with them is essential. It may be that they are aware of their child's ability but are unsure how to help him or her to develop it further.

In your role as coordinator it is a good idea to set up a meeting with particular parents and agree targets for the child in the same way the SENCO would do for a pupil with special needs. You can then set a review date and feedback to the parent on the child's progress. You can also offer the parent support and advice on how the pupil can make the most of his abilities. NAGC (National Association for Gifted Children) have a useful check list for home-school liaison:

- clear school policy on parent involvement
- friendly and approachable (not just on paper)
- parents' concerns always taken seriously
- regular feedback, not just end of term/year
- ways in which parents can help.

One boy at a Bedfordshire Middle School had a severe sight problem, which made it difficult for him to complete handwritten English tasks. Because of their own knowledge of the child, the parents believed he was capable of working at a higher level. Although initially there was poor communication between the parent and school, under the auspices of the SENCO and with the help of the boy's ICT teacher a solution was reached. For lessons where handwritten work was required the pupils was able to use a school laptop, similar to the one that his parents used with him at home. When exam practice was required and the pupil was due to take KS2 SATs where answers had to be handwritten, he was able to use a specially constructed desk, which altered the angle of his writing sufficiently for him to produce his best work. Happily, he achieved a high level in his English SATs test with an excellent score.

Home education

Parents who are not satisfied that the school is doing all it can to promote their child's abilities now have other options of which the home education movement is becoming an increasingly important one. In an article in *OM*, Kate Mosse, the author and founder of the Orange Prize for Fiction, said of her two children Martha and Felix, '...My husband and I are in favour of exams – and Felix will take them at 16 and 18, like Martha, but we were worried about the number of tests Felix was taking even at junior school, not least because of how much time was wasted preparing for tests rather than used for teaching. State education has become increasingly geared towards a narrow curriculum, leaving little time for improvisation...' Martha, 15, happily goes to school while Felix, 12, equally happily studies at home (France, 2005).

In my own experience, I can recall James, who was a pupil whose learning style did not suit the SATs approach. James was able and inventive with a fund of knowledge and ideas on scientific questions, and a love of improvisation in English. This brought excitement to class renditions of scenes from Macbeth. With his homemade cloak flying from his neck, James would proudly instruct Ross to '...pronounce his (the Thane of Cawdor's) present death, /And with his former title greet Macbeth...'.

Continual SATs practice in science and English wore him down, however, and from a bright start he became bored and listless. Eventually the parents found a group of adults in their own area who were committed to the idea of home education and James was enrolled with them. Their other child, however, like Kate Mosse's Martha, continued in his state school.

Incidentally, a year seven pupil who had just been reading the aforementioned *Skellig*, where Mina, one of the leading characters, is home educated, made the following very prescient remark in her review of the book:

> *'I think that home schooling is a great idea because the parents could teach the children what they want to know and need to know and give them the extra attention they need. And as for the pupils at local schools, there are so many rules and regulations and children can get taught things not wanted or not needed. And sometimes children can have friend problems, or get shouted at by a teacher when it is not necessary. Another problem with local schools is that the children could get too much homework. The drawback to home schooling is you need to be very well disciplined to actually sit down at home to work.'* (Lily, aged 12)

Handy Hints

- You may need to define talent for colleagues.
- Changing colleagues' thinking is important in ensuring that gifted and talented children are stretched sufficiently.
- Distribute and collect a staff questionnaire to see if the policy is working.
- Parents and carers may have and/or may welcome advice and suggestions.
- Home education may be an alternative for parents to consider.

CHAPTER 7

LOOKING AFTER YOURSELF

Looking after yourself as a gifted and talented coordinator shouldn't really be any different to just looking after yourself as a teacher. As it's a relatively new field, however, there are some things to look out for. First of all there's your job description. It could be as vague as, 'take responsibility for promoting issues regarding the more able and gifted pupils' or it could be far more detailed. *Box 7.1* shows one adapted from a course I attended at Oxford Brookes University in 2001:

Box 7.1 Suggested Job Description – Able Pupil Coordinator

1. Formulate, evaluate and revise able pupil policy:
   i. organising/chairing meetings
   ii. reviewing policy
   iii. identify areas for development such as INSET
2. Assist staff in identification and determining needs of individual pupils.
3. To maintain awareness of current trends/initiatives within the LEA; available INSET; and to disseminate information to staff as required.
4. To liaise with staff, parents, local schools, other professionals and the wider community.
5. To assist staff in planning to meet the needs of individual children and in monitoring of teaching and learning objectives.
6. To initiate and monitor the provision of extra-curricular activities aimed at enriching the learning experience of able pupils.

Second, you have to remember that gifted and talented should be a whole school policy and that you are not responsible for doing every part of it. One coordinator at a secondary school, who was also the Head of Geography, left identification and provision completely in the hands of the other heads of department, leaving her free to monitor the progress of individual pupils by setting up interviews with them and discussing whether they felt they were fulfilling the potential that had been highlighted.

Responsibility payments

It is rare that the gifted and talented coordinator is completely free of other responsibilities, especially at smaller schools and there is also rarely any extra money forthcoming for the post. In pre TLR (Teaching and Learning Responsibility payment) it was possible in some schools to receive a management allowance point for the post and also before the introduction of planning, preparation and assessment (PPA) it was possible to be given extra non-contact time in to enable coordinators to work with pupils and staff. Now anything more than the mandatory allowances will have to be negotiated separately with the headteacher. You could ask for an extra hour on top of the PPA time to help you to fulfil your role but you are unlikely to receive a responsibility payment. The head might even decide to link the gifted and talented role to that of the SENCO.

Allies

You will need to have at least one sympathetic colleague on the staff to whom you can look for support and advice when the going starts becoming uphill. A way of doing this is for you to encourage members of staff to make it part of their performance management. The author, who was a team leader at his school, worked with a colleague who was deeply interested in the gifted and talented idea. Her lessons were observed for performance management and she was encouraged to go on a course to improve her awareness of gifted and talented provision. This she did and was soon able to lead INSET on pupil identification at the school, leaving the author feeling less isolated in the sometimes challenging task of carrying the whole initiative himself.

Work–life balance

If you simply need to deal with your work–life balance and decide how much input you are going to make, there are a number of things you can do like refine your role, make sure you have time out with family and friends and get plenty of exercise – there's nothing like it for replenishing the grey cells.

In their excellent book, *Managing Teacher Workload*, Sarah Bubb and Peter Earley (2004) talk about effective leadership and management. This can be applied to your role because you are effectively a middle manager. Bubb and Earley stress the importance of:

- Staff helping to shape the school's aspirations and feeling more committed as a result.
- Presenting change in a positive light as a potential benefit to the school.
- Having a clear definition of the role and responsibility of coordinators.

Similarly, issues like managing meetings are dealt with under headings such as 'Calling the meeting – do you need to?', 'Setting the agenda – who is responsible for each item?',

'Taking the minutes – who will take action?' and 'Chairing skills – attending to the timing'. No one likes meetings that simply drag on without real purpose.

As you are likely to be in the coordinator's role because of your interest in gifted and talented issues you must ensure it doesn't take you over and getting your work–life balance right is a key issue here.

One teacher who had been a coordinator, a deputy, a head and finally, chief adviser in Luton, never allowed anything to go in his diary for Monday evening. The reason was that he and a teaching friend always went swimming on that evening. They kept up their routine at the same pool in Milton Keynes for over 20 years, using it as an opportunity to talk and joke about the successes and frustrations of the working week. The pool attendants would not have been born when they started!

Dealing with the uphill bit

Stephen Russell (1998), otherwise known as 'The Barefoot Doctor', used to run a column in a Sunday newspaper giving advice on how to handle life's up and down hills. One method that he recommends for dealing with external pressure, even in the midst of a busy day, is to spend 20 minutes sitting comfortably with eyes three quarters closed and to indulge in a form of meditation derived from the ancient Chinese-Taoist system. Like many such ideas it does work as a way of slowing you down.

Exercise is, of course, also to be recommended as a way of handling the stresses of a busy working life. And that doesn't mean just plodding round the block in your trainers on your own in the morning. Like most things, it's much more fun with other people and many schools will have the facilities – a hall or gym, equipment, even showers if you want. One school ran fitness classes each week for its staff; another had a volleyball class after work on a Friday which then got together with other schools to play at a more competitive level.

Although there are numerous other sources of advice on dealing with the demands of the job, Jill Parkin (2004), in an article in the *TES* about sharing problems, sums it up by saying:

- manage workload and time off
- take breaks
- don't stay late *and* take work home – one or the other
- give yourself time to think – it's okay to say no
- ask for help
- make time for yourself and your family and friends
- find what helps you relax.

THE FUTURE

Looking after yourself is also thinking about the future of your role as the gifted and talented coordinator. At the moment it looks very exciting. NAGTY have recently sent to all secondary schools information about how to enrol pupils on their database. This is aimed at pupils in the top five per cent of the ability range and involves the coordinator selecting pupils using a variety of means. It includes using national test results but you can also give references for pupils, which contain evidence of outstanding potential or achievement that has not been demonstrated by test scores.

NAGTY are aiming to be as inclusive as possible and writing about the English model of gifted and talented education, Deborah Eyre (2004) sets out a real vision for the future. She stresses that gifted education should be available to all, regardless of wealth or social background, saying that in this model the approach is integrated into general educational policy and that the approach itself integrates pupils with their peers. Although the material referred to is aimed at secondary schools, the English model contains a clear commitment to children in the primary age range.

Eyre goes on to say that there should be a high quality, basic system in which pupils can develop their gifts through normal class, cross school and out of school provision, and that there should be a balance between equality and meritocracy. In summary she says:

The English model of gifted education seeks to enable gifted and talented pupils from all backgrounds to fulfil their potential. England sees this as important if it is to:

- meet the challenge of globalization
- tackle inequality in the education system
- reflect social and cultural diversity
- lever up standards in general education.

The potential offered by this kind of approach is considerable:

- It is a relatively inexpensive option.
- It can be a lever to help raise standards in education generally.
- It supports the vulnerable especially the intelligent from under-represented groups.
- It provides a way to innovate teaching and learning and so is attractive to teachers.
- It addresses the 'geographical lottery' of provision.

Professor Eyre finishes her explanation of the model by saying that it is a radical approach, which depends on the whole teaching profession to make it work. She emphasises that a considerable change in culture is required to enable gifted education to become a vehicle for achieving excellence in the education system. It is hoped that this book will help you, the gifted and talented coordinator, to make this possible.

Handy Hints

- A job description is important both for you and for the other staff.
- Don't underestimate the importance of friends and allies.
- Some suggestions are given for managing the role.
- A radical future vision for all schools is given in the English model of gifted education (Eyre, 2004).

BIBLIOGRAPHY

REFERENCES

Almond D (1998) *Skellig.* Hodder Children's Books, London

Bleiman B, Webster L (2001) *The Poetry Book.* English and Media Centre, London

Bloom B, ed. (1956) *Taxonomy of Educational Objectives.* Vol. 1. Longman, Harlow

Bubb S, Earley P (2004) *Managing Teacher Workload.* Paul Chapman Publishing, London

Burke C, Grosvenor I (2003) *The School I'd Like.* RoutledgeFalmer, London

Carnell E (2004) *It's Like Mixing Colours.* ATL, London

Chapman A (2003) *Exploring G&T Transition.* National Primary Trust, Birmingham

Claxton G (2005) *An Intelligent Look at Emotional Intelligence.* ATL, London

Csikszentmihalyi M, Rathunde K, Whalen S (1997) *Talented Teenagers: The Roots of Success and Failure.* Cambridge University Press, Cambridge

Denscombe M (1998) *The Good Research Guide.* Open University Press, Buckingham

Department for Education and Skills (DfES) (2004) KS3 National Strategy *Key messages for teaching able, gifted and talented pupils.* DfES, London

Duffy FM (2003) I think therefore I am resistant to change. *Journal of National Staff Development Council* **24(1):** 30–6

Ellis T, McWhirter J, McColgan D, Haddow B (1977), *William Tyndale, the Teachers' Story*. Writers and Readers Publishing Co-operative, London

Eyre D (1997) *Able Children in Ordinary Schools*. David Fulton, London

Eyre D (2004) *Gifted Education: The English Model in Full National Academy for Gifted and talented Youth*. Available from: http://www.nagty.ac.uk/about/english_model_full.aspx

France L (2005) A class of their own. *OM* **17 April** (http://observer.guardian.co.uk/magazine/story/0,,1459735,00.html)

Freeman J (2001) *Gifted Children Grown Up*. David Fulton, London

Galton M, Gray J, Rudduck J (1999) *The Impact of School Transitions and transfers on Pupil Progress and Attainment*. Research Report RR131. DfEE Publications, Nottingham

Gardiner T (2003) It could be them. *TES Teacher* **19 September**

Gardner H (1983) *Frames of Mind: the Theory of Multiple Intelligences*. Basic Books, NY

Harlen W (1992) *The Teaching of Science, studies in primary education*. David Fulton, London

Hargreaves D (2004) *Working Laterally: How Innovation Networks Make an Education Epidemic*. DfES, London

Herrmann N (1988) *The Creative Brain*. Brain Books, Lake Lure, North Carolina

House of Commons Education and Employment Committee (1999) *Highly Able Children*. HMSO, London

Leyden S (2002) *Supporting the Child of Exceptional Ability*. David Fulton, London

Leyland P (2003) Raising motivation and achievement through groupwork. *G&T Update* **8:** 4–8

MacGilchrist B, Myers K, Reed J (2004) *The Intelligent School.* 2nd edn. Sage Publications, London

Murris K (2000) Can children do philosophy? *Journal of Philosophy of Education* **34(2):** 261–79

Noble C, Bradford B (2000) *Getting it right for boys... and girls.* Routledge, London and New York

Ofsted (2001) *Providing for gifted and talented pupils, an evaluation of the Excellence in Cities programme.* HMI, London

Oxford Brookes University (2001) *Guidelines for Nominal Group Techniques.* Oxford Brookes University, Oxford

Parkin J (2004) Stressed to the limit. *TES* **11 June**

Qualifications and Curriculum Authority (2000) *Science scheme of work for KS1 and KS2.* Department for Education and Employment, Nottingham

Renzulli JS, Rees SM (1985) *The Schoolwide Enrichment Model.* Creative Learning Press, Mansfield Center, CT

Russell S (1998) *Handbook for the Urban Warrior – a spiritual survival guide.* Piatkus, London

Teare B (1999) *Effective Resources for Able and Talented Children.* Network Educational Press Ltd, Stafford

Thorpe V, Asthana A (2005) In this school, the classroom revolution is now a reality – all 360 degrees of it. *Observer* **27 February** (http://observer.guardian.co.uk/uk_news/story/0,,1426369,00.html)

Winstanley C (2004) *Too Clever By Half.* Trentham Books, Stoke On Trent

FURTHER READING

Freeman J (1996) *Highly Able Girls and Boys.* DfEE, London

Freeman J (1998) *Educating the Very Able: Current International Research.* The Stationery Office, London

Leyland P (2004) Expecting to fly, or how I tried to disseminate ideas regarding G&T provision. *G&T Update* **19:** 4–5

Wallace B (2002) *Teaching Thinking Skills Across the Early Years.* David Fulton, London

USEFUL ADDRESSES

National Association for Able Children in Education
PO Box 242
Arnolds Way
Oxford OX2 9FR
http://www.nace.co.uk

National Association for Gifted Children (NAGC)
Suite 14, 2nd Floor, Challenge House
Sherwood Drive
Bletchley
Milton Keynes
Bucks MK3 6DP
http://www.nagcbritain.org.uk/

MENSA Foundation for Gifted Children
Mensa House
St John's Square
Wolverhampton WV2 4AH
www.mensa.org.uk

GIFT Ltd
24 Martingale Road
Billericay
Essex CM11 1SG

The Potential Trust
7 Shepherds Close
Kingston Stert, Nr Chinnor
Oxfordshire OX9 4NL

World Council for Gifted and Talented Children
210 Lindquist Centre
The University of Iowa
Iowa City, Iowa
52242-1529
USA

WEBSITES

Bigfoot Theatre Company
www.bigfoot-theatre.co.uk

Brunel Able Children's Centre (BACE)
www.brunel.ac.uk

Centre for Research in Mathematics
www.soton.ac.uk

Department for Education and Skills (DfES)
www.dfes.gov.uk

National Academy for Gifted and Talented Youth (NAGTY)
http://www.nagty.ac.uk

MA Education Ltd
www.markallengroup.com/education/

National Foundation for Educational Research (NFER)
www.nfer.ac.uk

Office for Standards in Education (England) (Ofsted)
www.ofsted.gov.uk

Optimus Publishing
www.optimuspub.co.uk

Westminster Institute of Education – Gifted and Talented
Professional Development
**http://www.brookes.ac.uk/schools/education/
rescon/cpdgifted/home.html!**